W9-CDI-231

No Lex 11-12

Famous Explorers

Henry Hudson

Claude Hurwicz

The Rosen Publishing Group's
PowerKids Press™
New York

To Amy Hurwicz and Gregory Hurwicz

Published in 2001 by The Rosen Publishing Group, Inc.
29 East 21st Street, New York, NY 10010

Photo Credits: Cover and title page © North Wind Pictures; p. 2 © Art Resource; pp. 2, 3 © SuperStock; pp. 2, 3, 16, 20 © The Granger Collection, New York; p. 4 © The Huntington Library, Art Collections, and Botanical Gardens, San Marino, CA/SuperStock; p. 6 © Archive Photos; pp. 1, 7, 8, 11, 12, 22 © North Wind Picture Archives; p. 15 © CORBIS/Bettmann; p. 19 (map) © North Wind Picture Archives, (iceberg) © Archive Photos; p. 23 © Tate Gallery, London/Art Resource, NY.

First Edition

Book Design: Maria E. Melendez and Felicity Erwin

Hurwicz, Claude.
    Henry Hudson / Claude Hurwicz.
      p. cm.—(Famous explorers)
    Includes index.
    Summary: This is a biography of the English explorer who hoped to find a northern route to the Far East and who explored North American waterways known today as the Hudson River, Hudson Bay, and Hudson Strait.
    ISBN 0-8239-5561-3 (alk. paper)
    1. Hudson, Henry, d. 1611—Juvenile literature. 2. America—Discovery and exploration—English—Juvenile literature.
3. Explorers—America—Biography—Juvenile literature. 4. Explorers—England—Biography—Juvenile literature. [1. Hudson, Henry, d. 1611. 2. Explorers. 3. America—Discovery and exploration—English.] I. Title. II. Series.

E129.H8 H87 2000
910'.92—dc21   00-026962
[B]

Manufactured in the United States of America

Contents

Europe

The Orient

A Short Route to the Orient

Henry Hudson was born in England in the 1570s. During this time, people from Europe were earning money by trading European goods for spices in the **Orient**. The Orient is made up of many countries in east and southeast Asia. The trips from England to the Orient took a long time. Ships had to travel through storms and around the southern tips of Africa or South America. Countries such as Portugal and Spain controlled these **routes** and made it hard for others to use them. English and Dutch trading companies sent explorers like Henry Hudson to find a shorter and safer route. Finding such a route became Hudson's dream.

This map was drawn by an artist in the 1500s. It shows what some people thought the routes to the Orient looked like.

A Life at Sea

Not much is known about Henry Hudson's early life. It is believed that as a young man he sailed to the Baltic Sea, the Mediterranean Sea, and around Africa. In 1607, the Muscovy Company, an English trading company, hired Hudson to be the **captain** of a small ship. The Muscovy Company wanted Hudson to find a **passage** to the Orient by way of the Arctic Ocean. This meant that Hudson would have to sail near the North Pole. Many countries, including Holland, had sent sailors to explore this route. No one had discovered a passage, though.

This is a picture of an English ship in the 1600s. In 1607, Hudson was hired by the Muscovy Company to find a faster route to the Orient.

7.

Hudson's 1st Journey

North Pole

Spitzbergen

Greenland

Iceland

England

The Hopewell

On May 1, 1607, Hudson and his son, John, and a crew of 10 men set sail from London on a ship called the *Hopewell*. They sailed northward, passing Iceland and reaching the eastern coast of Greenland. Then Hudson turned northeast toward the North Pole. There was too much ice for the *Hopewell* to continue. The ship had to change direction to the east.

In June Hudson reached the Svalbard Islands in the Arctic Ocean. The sea was full of whales that rubbed up against the ship. By August the *Hopewell* was blocked by ice again and had to turn around. The Arctic Ocean had not been fully explored by sailors yet, so people did not know that ice blocked the water. Hudson had gotten close to the North Pole. No ship had sailed so far north before.

This map shows Hudson's first voyage. The Hopewell *and its crew sailed to the northeast in search of a route across the Arctic Ocean to the Orient.*

Another Voyage on the *Hopewell*

Hudson and the *Hopewell* returned to England. The Muscovy Company sent Hudson and his crew on a second **voyage** to find a shorter route to the Orient. Hudson wanted to go north of Russia and around the eastern part of the North Pole. An explorer named Sir Hugh Willoughby had tried to go this way in 1553. Willoughby and his crew became trapped by ice and froze to death. Determined, Hudson set sail in April 1608. In May the *Hopewell* passed by the northern coast of Norway and through the Barents Sea. The crew had to watch for **icebergs**. At the end of June, the ship reached the Novaya Zemlya Islands. The *Hopewell* soon became blocked by ice. Hudson had failed in his mission again. He had no choice but to return home.

This map shows the route of Hudson's second voyage to reach the Orient. Icebergs, also called ice islands, were often spotted by the crew. If the ship hit an iceberg, it would be wrecked.

Hudson's 2nd Journey

England

Norway

Novaya Zemlya Islands

The Half Moon

The Muscovy Company considered Hudson's second voyage a failure. Hudson moved to Holland and asked the Dutch East India Company, another trading company, to pay for his second exploration of the Novaya Zemlya Islands. In April 1609, Hudson set sail from Amsterdam on a ship called the *Half Moon*.

Soon the *Half Moon* could no longer travel. The cold weather was hard on the crew and ice blocked the ship. The crew wanted to return home. Instead Hudson headed toward North America. He believed that there was a river that went from the Atlantic Ocean to the Pacific Ocean. The *Half Moon* headed west in search of the river.

The Half Moon *left the port in Amsterdam, Holland, in April 1609 for Hudson's third voyage. Hudson's crew included English and Dutch sailors.*

13

North America and Its People

On July 17, 1609, the *Half Moon* arrived in North America on the coast of what is today the state of Maine. On their way south along the coast, Hudson and his men met many Native Americans. They were friendly and wanted to trade with the visitors. Even though the crew had been welcomed by Native Americans, some of the sailors attacked the Native Americans and stole from them.

Hudson continued to look for a river that would lead him west across America to the Pacific Ocean. He headed south, down the coast to Virginia. Then he turned around and sailed north to explore the bays now known as Chesapeake Bay and Delaware Bay. He still hoped to fulfill his life's dream of finding a shorter route to the Orient.

The Half Moon *sailed across the Atlantic from Holland. Hudson hoped to find a water passage in America that would lead to the Pacific Ocean. He traded with the Native Americans he met in America.*

1609

The Hudson River

Hudson and the crew of the *Half Moon* arrived at what we now call New York in September 1609. There, Hudson began his most famous trip, sailing up the river that is now named the Hudson River.

The Native American men they met along the Hudson River wore feathers. The Native American women wore copper jewelry. Hudson received gifts of tobacco, traded knives and beads, and visited a village. Even though the crew had some friendly meetings with the Native Americans, other Native Americans attacked Hudson's crew as they went up the river. The *Half Moon* kept moving up the river looking for a way to the Pacific Ocean. Hudson could not find one. At the time, he felt this trip was a failure. We now know that Hudson discovered New York and the Hudson River for Holland.

In 1609, Hudson explored New York Bay and the river that today has his name. The Half Moon *sailed as far as what is now the city of Albany.*

17

The Discovery

By the end of 1609, Hudson and his crew had decided to return to England instead of Holland. Then on April 17, 1610, Hudson set sail again from England in a new ship called the *Discovery*. He was still searching for a shorter route to the Orient. By June 25, 1610, the *Discovery* had entered what is now called the Hudson **Strait**. This waterway connects the Atlantic Ocean with what is now Hudson Bay. The entrance to the strait was called the Furious Overfall. It was very dangerous because of rushing tides, **whirlpools**, icebergs, and thick fog. The ship was often trapped by ice and the men were running out of food.

A French map from the 1700s shows the Hudson Bay. Hudson had led the Discovery out of the ice, but his crew was scared and wanted to turn back.

Pays Inconnus

Cap Bleu

milles Isles

Cap aux Vaches marines

I. Natingan

I. Salbre

DETROIT D HVDSON

I. Phelipeaux ou Mansfeld

BAYE

I. du point du jour

Cap aigres

I. du Cap Charles

Cap Haut

Pais des

Esquimaux

Monsipi ou Danoire

R. Bourbon
R Bourbon

R. S. Therese

I. de la Trinité

D HVD

de nieuse

SON

I. Plex

I. agamesque

I. Titele

I. Charleston

I. Petit Bois

R. nemisco

R. Monsipi ou Arue

R. aux Iroquois

19

Hudson Bay and Mutiny

On August 2, 1610, the *Discovery* entered what is now Hudson Bay. Hudson ordered the crew to sail south. He hoped to find warmer waters and a way to the Pacific Ocean. By November the *Discovery* was at the southern end of the bay, but it was frozen because of the winter weather. The land around Hudson Bay was ice, dirt, and rock. There were no plants or animals for food. The men were becoming angry with Hudson. Many got sick and some even died. On June 21, 1611, the crew could no longer wait for Hudson to order their return home. They decided to start a **mutiny**. On June 24, the **mutineers** threw Hudson, his son, and seven others onto a rowboat without food or water. Hudson was not seen or heard from again.

Henry Hudson, his son, and seven other loyal sailors, were cast overboard in a rowboat by mutineers in June 1611.

After the Mutiny

The **surviving** mutineers returned to England. They were not **punished** for taking part in a mutiny.

As for Henry Hudson and the others, some say they made it to shore. There are legends that Hudson's ghost roams the **regions** he explored. Today Henry Hudson is best remembered for being a great **navigator**, and for discovering and exploring the Hudson River, Hudson Strait, and Hudson Bay.

Henry Hudson's Timeline

1607–Hudson makes his first voyage to find a shorter passage to the Orient.

1609–Hudson explores a river in North America. It is later named the Hudson River.

1610–Hudson explores what is today the Hudson Strait and Hudson Bay.

1611–Hudson's men take part in a mutiny.

Glossary

captain (KAP-ten) The leader of a ship.

icebergs (IYS-burgz) Very large pieces of ice floating in the water.

mutineers (myoo-ten-EERZ) People who disobey the captain on a ship.

mutiny (MYOO-tin-ee) Disobeying a captain's orders.

navigator (NA-vuh-gay-tur) An explorer of the seas.

Orient (OR-ee-ent) The east and southeast part of the world on the continent of Asia. It is also called the Far East.

passage (PAS-ij) A way along which one can pass.

punished (PUN-isht) To have caused pain or loss to someone for a crime they have committed.

regions (REE-jens) Different parts of the earth.

routes (ROOTS) Paths taken to get somewhere.

strait (STRAYT) A narrow waterway connecting two large bodies of water.

surviving (sur-VYV-ing) Staying alive.

voyage (VOY-ij) A journey by water.

whirlpools (WURL-poolz) Water that moves in circles, creating holes in the middle that suck things into them.

Index

Web Sites

To learn more about Henry Hudson, check out these Web sites:
http://www.ianchadwick.com/hudson/
http://www.mariner.org/age/hudson.html